WACKY JOKES

This book belongs to

_____

_____

MARKS &
SPENCER

Illustrated by Leighton Noyes
Written by Sandy Ransford

Marks and Spencer p.l.c.
PO Box 3339
Chester CH99 9QS

s h o p   o n l i n e
www.marksandspencer.com

Copyright © Exclusive Editions 2007
ISBN 1-84461-828-5
Printed in China

Contents

Goofy Giggles

What kind of crisps
can fly?
Plain ones.

What would you do if you
met a group of aliens
walking down the road?
**Hope they were going
to a fancy dress party!**

What has 20 legs,
but can't walk?
Ten pairs of trousers.

What is round, white
and smells awful?
A ping-pong ball.

What grows on
www.fields.com and stings?
Internettles.

Why are goldfish red ?
The water turns them rusty!

Why did the elephant paint
its toenails red?
**So it could hide in a
strawberry patch.**

Have you ever seen
an elephant in a
strawberry patch?
**Shows what a good
disguise it is, doesn't it!**

How can you tell if an
elephant's been in your fridge?
**By the footprints
in the butter.**

How does an elephant
climb a tree?
**Sits on an acorn and
waits for it to grow.**

How does an elephant
come down a tree?
**Sits on a leaf and
waits for autumn.**

"Did you hear the joke
about the butter?"
"No, what is it?"
**"I'd better not tell you,
you might spread it around."**

How do you make a
banana split?
Cut it in two.

How do you make an
apple puff?
**Chase it round
the garden.**

"Why did you park
your car here?"
**"Because the sign says
Fine for Parking."**

Two flies were playing football
in a saucer. One said to the other,
"We'll have to do better than
this, we're playing in the
cup next week."

Which football team spends
all its spare time
at pop concerts?
Blackburn Ravers.

What's the definition
of a teacher?
**Someone who talks in
someone else's sleep.**

Why do giraffes have
such long necks?
Because their feet smell.

Why did the snail start to climb an apple tree in the spring?

Because by the time it got up there, the apples would be ready to eat!

What's tall and wet and stands in the middle of Paris?

The Eiffel Shower.

Which country has no fat people?

Finland.

What's worse than biting into an apple and finding a maggot?

Biting into an apple and finding half a maggot!

What can you do if you get locked out of your house?

Sing until you find the right key.

What do you get if you cross a cat with a lemon?

A sourpuss.

What do you get if you cross a cow with a duck?
Cream quackers.

What do you get if you cross a chicken with a cement mixer?
A bricklayer.

What's yellow, red and white and flies at 500mph?
A pilot's egg and tomato sandwich.

When do elephants have 20 feet?
When there are five of them.

How do you stop a herd of elephants charging?
Take away their credit cards.

What's the best way
to raise an elephant?
With a fork-lift truck.

How do you get an
elephant in a matchbox?
**Take out the
matches first.**

Where do pigs go
when they die?
To the sty in the sky.

Why did the farmer
call his pig 'Ink'?
**It was always running
out of the pen.**

How do you count cows?
With a cowculator.

Why did the egg go
to the North Pole?

**Because it was an
egg-splorer.**

Why do worms taste
like chewing-gum?

Because they're wrigglies.

What did the bee say
to the wasp?

**"I must fly now,
but I'll give you a
buzz later."**

What happens to cows
in hot weather?
**They give
evaporated milk.**

What did the boy centipede
say to the girl centipede?
**"May I hold your
hand, hand, hand..."**

If a sheep says 'Moo,'
instead of 'Baa,'
what does it mean?
**It's learning a
foreign language.**

What do you get if you cross
a sheep with a thunderstorm?
A wet blanket.

What did the horse say
when it finished it's dinner?
"This is the last straw."

Why can't horses dance?
**Because they have
two left feet.**

Have you read:
'Keep on Trying' by Percy Vere
'Picking Up Litter' by Phil D. Basket
'Light Lunches' by Roland Butter
'How to Get Rich' by Robin Banks
'Crossing the Desert'
by Rhoda Camel

Which part of a car is the laziest?
The wheels.
They're always tyred.

What do athletes enjoy eating?
Runner beans.

What should you do
with a green car?
Wait until it ripens.

Knock, knock.
Who's there?
Justin.
Justin who?
Justin time for tea.

What do you call the Star Wars
character who spends his time
walking into the sea?
Darth Wader.

Why is grass dangerous?
**Because it's full
of blades.**

Where do you find
giant snails?
**On the ends of
giants' fingers.**

What's yellow and has
a very long neck?
A giraff-odil.

What's yellow and very silly?
A daft-odil.

What can fly underwater?
**A bluebottle in
a submarine.**

Two fleas were on their
way into town.
"Shall we walk?" asked one.
**"No," said the second.
"Let's take a dog."**

How did the two fleas
travel from London
to Edinburgh?
By itch-hiking.

Did you hear what
happened to the flea circus?
**A dog came along
and stole the show!**

Where's the best place to go
dancing in California?
San Frandisco.

What happens if you dial 666?

Three policemen come along walking on their heads.

What's an American cow's favourite city?

Moo York.

What's an American hen's favourite city?

Chickago.

How do you get a baby
astronaut to go to sleep?
Rocket.

How can you identify a
baby snake?
By its rattle.

When is it bad luck
to see a black cat?
When you're a mouse.

What did the mouse say
when it broke its front teeth?
"Hard cheese."

What do you get if you cross
a mouse with an elephant?
**Enormous holes in the
skirting-board!**

Did you hear the story about the three holes in the ground?
Well, well, well.

What keeps hot in the fridge?
Mustard.

What was King Arthur's favourite game?
Knights and crosses.

Why is history the sweetest lesson?
Because it is full of dates.

Where do tadpoles change into frogs?
In a croakroom.

What goes in pink
and comes out blue?
A swimmer in winter.

Where did the astronaut
leave his spaceship?
At a parking meteor.

What is an astronaut's
favourite meal?
Launch.

What's grey, has four legs
and a trunk?
A mouse going on holiday.

How can you stop
fish from smelling?
Cut off their noses.

Knock, knock.
Who's there?
Dismay.
Dismay who?
**Dismay be an alien,
don't open the door!**

Knock, knock.
Who's there?
Norma Lee.
Norma Lee who?
**Norma Lee I live on
Mars but I'm visiting
Earth today!**

"Have you ever seen
a catfish?"
"Yes."
"How did it hold the rod?"

What's the difference between
a fish and a piano?
You can't tuna fish.

Who invented fire?
Oh, some bright spark.

How can you start
a fire with two sticks?
**Make sure one of
them is a match!**

"Don't go near the pond,
it's very deep."
**"But it can't be that
deep, Mum. It only
reaches up to the middle
of those ducks."**

What happens to a duck
before it grows up?
It grows down.

Where did Noah keep
his bees?
In the ark hives.

What did Noah do
when it got dark?
**Switched on the
floodlights.**

What do you call a man with
a paper bag on his head?
Russell.

Why did the little boy
paddle in his socks?
The water was cold.

What trees grow near
the seaside?
Beech trees.

What happens if
you walk under a cow?
**You might get a
pat on the head.**

Why do cows lie
down close together?
To keep each udder warm.

What do you call two
turnips who fall in love?
Swedehearts.

What do elephants
do in the back of a Mini?
Play squash.

Where are whales weighed?
**At a whale-weigh
station.**

Why are sausages bad-mannered?
**Because they spit in the
frying-pan.**

What was green and used
to hold up stage coaches?
Dick Gherkin.

What do jelly babies
wear on their feet?
Gum boots.

What do you call an
exploding monkey?
A ba-boom!

What's the fittest
animal in the jungle?
A gym-panzee.

What did the alien say
to the gardener?
**Take me to
your weeder.**

What did one comet
say to another?
Pleased to meteor.

What has six eyes
but cant see?
The Three Blind Mice.

How do you hire a horse?
Stand it on four bricks.

"I'd like a hair-cut, please"
**"Certainly, sir,
which one?"**

What disappears when
you put the light on?
Darkness!

"Where do you swim?"
"In the spring."
"I said where, not when!"

What's a horse's
favourite game?
Stable tennis.

How can you keep cool
at a football match?
Sit next to a fan.

What do you say to a
dead robot?
Rust in peace!

Why don't aliens celbrate
Christmas?
**Beacause they don't like to
give away their presence.**

A boy went swimming and
when he got out of the water
he found all his clothes
had been stolen.
What did he go home in?
The dark!

"Is this river good for fish?"
**"It must be, because
I've never managed
to persuade any to come
out of it!"**

I eat my peas with honey,
I've done it all my life.
It makes the peas taste funny
But it keeps them on the knife!

Why do people play
football?
For kicks.

"Is that bull safe?"
**"He's a lot safer
than you are!"**

When are most
frogs born?
In a leap year.

"How did Mum know
you hadn't washed?"
"I forgot to wet the towel."

"Where are you from?"
"Scotland."
"What part?"
"All of me."

Where do monkeys pick
up wild rumours?
On the apevine.

How do monkeys
get down the stairs?
**They slide down
the banana-ster.**

"Dad, a man called to
see you when you were out."

"Did he have a bill?"

**"No, just an ordinary
nose like everybody else."**

What do you call a
dog with a cold?

A choo-wawa.

What do you call a
smelly fairy?

Stinkerbell.

What did the policeman
say to his belly button?

"You're under a vest."

What do dinosaurs use
to cut down trees?

Dinosaws!

"I'd like an elephant sandwich, please."

"I'm sorry, we don't do elephant sandwiches."

"Why not?"

"We haven't any bread."

"If you eat any more you'll burst!"

"Then you'd better watch out, because I'm going to have some pudding!"

"Mum, will you do my homework for me, please?"

"No, it wouldn't be right."

"But you could at least try!"

"That's a funny pair of socks, one red and one blue!"

"Yes, and I've got another pair at home just like it."

What lives in the sea and carries people from place to place?
An octobus!

What's the fastest gorilla in the jungle?
King Kong-cord.

Horribly Horrid

What do vampires like for breakfast?
Ready Neck.

What did the mummy mummy say to her little girl one cold winter's morning?
"Wrap up well, dear."

"Doctor, I think I've been bitten by a vampire."
"Drink this glass of water."
"Will it make me better?"
"No, but I'll be able to see if your neck leaks."

Where do vampires keep their money?
In blood banks.

What's a vampire's favourite fruit?
A blood orange.

How can you join Dracula's fan club?
Send your name, address and blood group.

Why don't skeletons go
to discos?
**They have no body
to dance with.**

What do you get if Batman and
Robin are run over
by a steamroller?
Flatman and Ribbon.

What's a baby zombie's
favourite toy?
A deady bear.

Why are mummies
good at keeping secrets?
**They keep everything
under wraps.**

What do you call a mummy
who eats biscuits in bed?
A crumby mummy.

What do mummies paint
on their fingers?
Nile varnish.

Why was the Ancient Egyptian
boy confused?
**Because his daddy
was a mummy.**

Where does an
undertaker work?
In a box office.

How does an undertaker
start a letter?
Tomb it may concern.

How do undertakers speak?
Gravely.

39

Why was the witch arrested
for speeding?
**She was riding her
broom-broomstick.**

How does an undertaker
tie his tie?
With a wreath knot.

What do you call a man
who's been buried for
thousands of years?
Pete.

Why do skeletons drink milk?
Because it's good for their bones.

What do skeletons have at their parties?
A rattling good time.

Why did the skeleton feel the cold so badly?
The wind blew straight through him.

What do you call a skeleton that's always asleep?
Lazy bones.

What do ghosts like for breakfast?
Dreaded Wheat.

Where does a ghost train stop?
At a manifestation.

Which ghost made friends
with the three bears?
Ghouldilocks.

Where do ghosts
like to swim?
In the Dead Sea.

What's a ghost's
favourite tree?
A ceme-tree.

What do short-sighted
ghosts wear?
Spooktacles.

What do Italian ghosts
like for supper?
Spook-hetti.

Why did the ghost
look in the mirror?
**To see if he still
wasn't there.**

Why was the
ghost arrested?
**He didn't have
a haunting licence.**

How does a ghost count to ten?
**One, boo, three, four,
five, six, seven,
hate, nine, frighten!**

What's a ghost's
favourite dessert?
Strawberries and scream.

What's the phantom
coast guard called?
The ghost guard.

What do you call a ghost that
haunts a hospital?
A surgical spirit.

Why couldn't the witch
write a letter?
**She was no good
at spelling.**

How does a witch
tell the time?
By her witch-watch.

What does a vampire have
at 11 o'clock every morning?
A coffin break.

Why don't vampires get fat?
**They eat necks
to nothing.**

Who won the monsters'
beauty contest?
No body!

What do monsters sing
at Christmas?
**"Deck the halls
with poison ivy ..."**

What are twin
vampires called?
Blood Brothers

How does a monster
count up to 30?
On its fingers.

What did the monster
say to its victim?
**"So long, it's been good
to gnaw you."**

What do you call a monster
with three eyes and
four mouths?
Very ugly!

How do you greet a
three-headed monster?
"Hello, hello, hello."

Knock, knock.

Who's there?

Donna.

Donna who?

Donna look now but there's a great big monster right behind you!

What day of the week
do monsters eat people?

Chewsday.

What do ghosts eat
with roast beef?

Grave-y.

What do phantom
football fans shout?

**"Here we ghost,
Here we ghost,
Here we ghost ..."**

What do sea monsters
like to eat?

Fish and ships.

What did the sea monster
say when it saw a submarine?
"Oh, good, tinned food."

What do country
monsters like to eat?
**Shepherd's pie, made
with real shepherds.**

How do monster snowmen
feel when they melt?
Abominable.

Have you seen an
Abominable Snowman?
Not yeti.

Why do monsters forget
what you tell them?
**Because it goes in
one ear and out of
all the others.**

How did Frankenstein's
monster eat his food?
He bolted it down.

How does a werewolf
sign his letters?
"Best vicious."

Why did the werewolf
jump in the washing-machine?
**It was a
wash-and-werewolf.**

What did Frankenstein's
monster say when he was
struck by lightning?
"I needed that."

Why was Dracula sad?
His love was in vein.

Why did Dracula use
special toothpaste?
He had bat breath.

What did Dracula say to his
victim after he bit her?
"Fangs very much."

What food was Dracula
afraid of?
Steak.

Why didn't Dracula
have many friends?
**He was a pain in
the neck.**

Where did Dracula go when he
visited New York?
The Vampire State Building.

Whom did Dracula marry?
The girl necks door.

Knock, knock.
Who's there?
Hugo.
Hugo who?
Hugo first, I'm frightened!

What do monsters eat
with bread and cheese?
Pickled organs.

What do baby monsters
say at bedtime?
"Read me a gory."

What do you get if you
cross a ghost with a sailor?
A sea ghoul.

What's a monster's
favourite football team?
Slitherpool.

What's a monster's
favourite ballet?
Swamp Lake.

Why do dragons
sleep in the daytime?
So they can fight knights.

What did the grown-up dragon
say to the baby dragon?
"You're too young to smoke."

What game do dragons
play at parties?
Swallow my leader.

"My dad has hundreds
of people under him."
"Really? What does he do?"
**"He cuts the grass in the
cemetery."**

"What's the world's
deadliest poison?"
"An aeroplane."
"What do you mean, an aeroplane?"
"One drop and you're dead."

How do you tell when a
corpse is angry?
It flips its lid.

Why were the skeleton's
teeth chattering?
**He was chilled to
the marrow.**

What do you get if you are hit
on the head with an axe?
A splitting headache.

What type of dog does
Dracula have?
A blood hound.

What happened when someone
hit the skeleton on his shins?
He hadn't a leg to stand on.

What did the monster
say to the piano?
**"What beautiful teeth
you've got. "**

What did the ghost teacher
say to her pupils?
**"Watch the board, children,
and I'll go through it again."**

What did the boy vampire say
to the glamorous girl vampire?
"Hello, gore-juice."

Where do skeletons
go on holiday?
The Ghosta Brava.

What do you call a
skeleton who's a friend?
A bony crony.

What's a monster's favourite TV programme?
Horror-nation Street.

"Did you know there's a new horror at the cinema this week?"
"Yes, I daren't buy a ticket from him. "

How does a ghost pass through a locked door?
He uses a skeleton key.

What do you get if you cross a skeleton with a python?
A rattlesnake.

"I think our school's haunted."
"Why?"
"Well, the head teacher's always talking about the school spirit. "

What does a ghost's bicycle have?
Spooks in its wheels.

Knock, knock.
Who's there?
Fred.
Fred who?
Fred of ghosts!

What do zombies
like for lunch?
Baked beings on toast.

What were the ghost's
earrings made from?
Tomb stones.

What did the zombie say when he
spotted the sleeping man?
**"Oh, good,
breakfast in bed."**

What happened to the
zombie after he ate the comedian?
**He got a funny feeling
in his stomach.**

What kind of beans do
zombies like to eat?
Human beans!

How does a zombie
greet a human being?
"Pleased to eat you."

What does a zombie
do at a wedding?
**Toasts the bride
and groom.**

Did you hear about the
zombie who went on a cruise ship?
**In the restaurant he refused
the menu and asked for the
passenger list.**

What did the zombie
write at Christmas?
His chopping list.

Why couldn't the witch
give a speech?
**She had a frog
in her throat.**

What screams more loudly
than a person frightened
by a witch?
**Two people frightened
by a witch!**

Where did the witch have
her hair done?
At the ugly parlour.

What does a witch do
on her broomstick?
Sweeps the sky.

How does a ghost keep
its feet dry in wet weather?
It wears ghouloshes.

Where does a ghost
send its laundry?
To the dry screamers.

What is a ghost's least
favourite saying?
"Never say die."

"I need a serious talk with you,"
said one graveyard worm to
another. "OK," replied his friend,
"let's go and talk in dead Ernest."

What game do ghosts
play at parties?
Haunt the thimble.

What pastimes did the country ghost enjoy?
Fishing, shooting and haunting.

Where do ghosts get their jokes from?
Crypt writers.

What do skeletons get on the Ghosta Brava?
A skele-tan.

Why do witches drink tea?
**Because sorcerers
need cuppas.**

How does a witch from
Mars travel around?
In a flying saucerer.

What happened when
the witch was ill?
**The doctor said she
could get up for a spell
when she felt better.**

"Our cat took first prize
at the bird show."
"How could a cat do that?"
**"Easy – he ate the
prize-winning canary."**

What do you get if you
cross the Atlantic with
the Titanic?
Halfway.

What do hangmen read?
Noosepapers.

"Doctor, doctor,
I'm at death's door!"
**"Don't worry, I'll pull you
through."**

"Doctor, doctor, I'm
having trouble breathing!"
**"Don't worry, I'll soon
put a stop to that!"**

"Doctor, doctor, my little boy
has just swallowed a bullet!"
"Well, don't point him at me!"

"What happened to the
woman the magician
sawed in half?"
**"She's now living in
London and Glasgow."**

"I'd like to book a box for four."
"Sorry, sir, we only have boxes for one."

"Is that the Empire Theatre?"
"No, it's the undertakers."

How did the skeleton know
it was going to rain?
He could feel it in his bones.

"Doctor, doctor, I feel half dead."
"Don't worry, I'll arrange for you to be buried from the waist up."

What's the best way to
talk to a vampire?
Long distance.

What does a fiend do
at the weekend?
Takes his girl-fiend to the cinema.

64

What is Dracular's
favourite fruit?
Neck-tarines.

What has four legs and flies?
A dead sheep.

Who's the most important
player in the ghosts'
football team?
The ghoul-keeper.

What do you get if
King Kong sits on your piano?
A flat note.

What is a vampire's
favourite kind of coffee?
De-coffin-ated!

What monster plays
the most April Fool's jokes?
Prankenstein.

What do ghosts
do at Christmas?
**Go to see a
phantomine.**

What do you call
a friendly monster?
A failure.

Why didn't the
skeleton go
bungee-jumping?
**He didn't have
the guts.**

What's a sea
monsters favourite meal?
Fish and ships.

What happened when
the wizard met the witch?
**It was love
at first fright.**

What is as sharp
as a vampire's fang?
His other fang.

Where do ghosts
go on holiday?
The Isle of Fright.

What do you call a
ghost who haunts
the town hall?
A night mayor.

What do vampires
read to their children
at night?
Bite-time stories.

Seriously Silly

What would you do with
a blue banana?
Try to cheer it up.

"Waiter! What kind of
soup is this?"

"It's bean soup, sir."

**"I don't care what it's
been, what is it now?"**

What sea creature
is good at maths?
An octoplus.

"Doctor, doctor, I keep thinking
I'm a sheep!"

"How do you feel?"

"Very baaaad."

"Why is your sister crying?"

"Because I won't give her
my piece of cake."

"Well, what happened to her
own piece of cake?"

**"She cried when I ate
that, too."**

Knock, knock.
Who's there?
Howard.
Howard who?
Howard I know?

What do you get if you cross
an elephant with a chicken?
**A creature that remembers
why it crossed the road.**

What do you get if you cross
a pig with a zebra?
Striped sausages.

If an apple a day keeps
the doctor away, what does
an onion a day do?
Keeps everyone away!

"I heard a new joke yesterday.
Did I tell you it?"
"Is it funny?"
"Yes."
"Then you didn't."

"Waiter! Do you have frogs' legs?"
**"No, sir, it's just the
way I walk."**

Did you hear the story
of the three eggs?
Too bad.

Why did the car get
a puncture?
**There was a fork
in the road.**

"Our dog can play chess."
"Really? He must be clever."
**"Oh, I don't know.
I usually win."**

What's the hardest thing
about learning to ride a horse?
The ground.

"What's frozen water?"

"Ice."

"And what's frozen tea?"

"Iced tea."

"And what's frozen ink?"

"Iced ink."

"I know you do!"

Why did the golfer wear an extra pair of trousers?

In case he got a hole in one.

Why do cows wear bells?

Because their horns don't work.

Knock, knock.

Who's there?

Police.

Police who?

**Police let me in,
it's cold out here.**

Knock, knock.

Who's there?

Ooze.

Ooze who?

**Ooze eaten all
the toffees?**

Knock, knock.

Who's there?

Felix.

Felix who?

**Felix my ice cream
again I'll thump him.**

If you have an umpire in
tennis, and a referee in
football, what do you have
in bowls?

Goldfish.

Who wrote
Embarrassing Moments?
Lucy Lastic.

"Doctor, doctor,
I keep thinking I'm a cat."
"How long has this
been going on?"
**"Ever since I
was a kitten."**

"Doctor, doctor,
I keep thinking I'm a dog."
"Come here and sit on a chair."
**"I can't, I'm not allowed
on the furniture."**

"Doctor, doctor, I keep
thinking I'm a canary."
**"Wait there and I'll tweet
you in a minute."**

What's yellow and
very dangerous?
Shark-infested custard.

Did you hear the story
about the peacock?
It's a wonderful tale.

"Waiter! There's a button
in my salad!"
**"Yes, sir, it's off the
jacket potato."**

What runs across the floor without any legs?

Water.

Why does a rabbit have a shiny nose?

Because it's powder puff is at the wrong end.

If a buttercup is yellow, what colour is a hiccup?

Burple.

Who wrote 'Making a Vegetable Garden'?

Rosa Carrots.

Who wrote 'Keeping Your Garden Tidy'?

Anita Lawn.

"I like your Easter tie."

"Why do you call it my Easter tie?"

"Because it's covered in egg."

What wobbles
when it flies?
A jellycopter.

What sits on the seabed
and shivers?
A nervous wreck.

Why do policemen who don't
wear uniforms belong to
the C.I.D.?
**Because it stands for
Coppers in Disguise.**

What did the lady say to
the man at the door with
a drum?
Beat it!

What did the boy say to
the man at the door with the
wooden leg?
Hop it!

What's white on the outside,
green on the inside, and hops?
A frog sandwich.

"I've lost my dog."

"Why don't you put an advertisement in the paper?"

"Don't be silly, my dog can't read."

What do you get if you cross a sheepdog with a bunch of roses?
Cauliflowers.

What do you get if you cross a sheepdog with a jelly?
Collie-wobbles.

What do you get if you cross a gun-dog with a telephone?
A golden receiver.

What would you do if an elephant sat in front of you at the cinema?
Miss most of the film.

"Waiter! This coffee tastes like mud!"

"I'm not surprised, sir, it was ground just a few minutes ago."

How can you tell a weasel from a stoat?

A weasel's weasily recognised, but a stoat's stoatally different.

What should you do if you lose your canary?

Inform the Flying Squad.

How do you get two whales in a Mini?

Over the Severn Bridge.

"Have you heard? The Police are looking for a man with one eye called Johnson."

"What's his other eye called?"

What are the best things to put in a Christmas cake?

Your teeth!

What did one tomato
say to the other?
**"You go on ahead
and I'll ketchup."**

What do you call an
American drawing?
A Yankee Doodle.

What do you get if you
pour boiling water down
a rabbit hole?
Hot, cross bunnies.

What do you get if you cross
a cat with a ball of wool?
Mittens.

Why do bees have sticky hair?
They use honey combs.

Who was the first
underwater spy?
James Pond.

"What did the tie say to
the hat?"
**"I'll hang around and
you go on ahead."**

Have you heard the
joke about the bed?
It hasn't been made yet.

Knock, knock.
Who's there?
Eddie.
Eddie who?
Eddie body home?

Knock, knock.
Who's there?
Barbara.
Barbara who?
**Barbara black sheep,
have you any wool?**

"Do you know how many sheep it takes to make one jumper?"
"No, I didn't even know sheep could knit."

Knock, knock.
Who's there?
Arfur.
Arfur who?
Arfur got.

"Have you been fighting again? You've lost a front tooth!"
"I haven't lost it, Mum, it's in my pocket."

What do cats read
at breakfast?
Mewspapers.

"Harold! Have you got
your shoes on yet?"
"Yes, Mum, all except one."

"You've got your socks
on inside out."
**"I know, but there are holes
on the other side."**

What does God have
for tea?
Angel cake.

What do elves have
for tea?
Fairy cakes.

What do you get if
you cross a bear with a skunk?
Winnie the Pooh.

"You remind me of Andy Jones."
"I'm not a bit like Andy Jones."
**"Yes, you are.
You both pinched
my football."**

"Share your sledge
with your little sister, Billy."
**"OK, Mum, she can have
it going uphill and I'll have
it going downhill."**

What's a fjord?
A Norwegian car.

Knock, knock.

Who's there?

Bertha.

Bertha who?

Happy Bertha-day!

Knock, knock.

Who's there?

Butter.

Butter who?

Butter be quick, I need to go to the loo.

Knock, knock.

Who's there?

Dishes.

Dishes who?

Dishes the police. Open the door!

"Was the scenery in Switzerland as beautiful as they say it is?"

"I don't know, I couldn't see it. There were too many mountains in the way."

"Why do you say your drum is the best present you ever had?"

"Mum gives me 50p a day not to play it."

What did the sea say to the shore?

Nothing, it just waved.

How can you tell which end of a worm is the head?

Tickle its middle and see which end smiles.

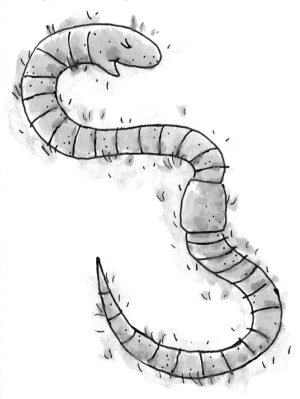

What do you call a
snowman in the Sahara?
A puddle.

What did the ram say
to the female sheep?
"After ewe."

What do female
sheep wear?
Eweniforms.

What do you call a
rabbit with fleas?
Bugs Bunny.

Which pantomime is about
a cat in a chemist's shop?
Puss in Boots.

Why was the centipede late
for the football match?
**It took him hours to
put his boots on.**

"Can you see into the future?"
"No."
**"Good. Then will you
lend me £13?"**

What's the difference
between a buffalo and a bison?
**You can't wash your
hands in a buffalo.**

What's the difference
between a dog and a flea?
**A dog can have fleas,
but a flea can't have dogs.**

How do you make
a bandstand?
Take away their chairs.

What does a pig use
to write a letter?
Pen and oink.

"It's raining cats and dogs!"
**"I know, I just stepped
in a poodle."**

What kind of dogs do
hairdressers have?
Shampoodles.

What happens when you put
the letter M in the fridge?
It changes ice into mice.

Why can't a car
play football?
**Because it's only
got one boot.**

What do you call two
banana skins?
A pair of slippers.

Which side of a cat
has the most fur?
The outside.

What can go up a chimney down,
but not down a chimney up?
An umbrella.

What's the safest way
to use a hammer?
**Get someone else
to hold the nails.**

What do you get if you cross a football team with an ice cream?
Aston Vanilla.

"Can you spell Mississippi?"
"Well, I can start, but I'm not sure I can finish!"

Does an apple a day keep the teacher away?
It does if your aim is good enough!

"What subjects are you studying for your exams?"
"French, Spanish and geometry."
"Where do they speak geometry?"

"What's half of 8?"
"Across or down?"
"What do you mean?"
"Well, across it's nought, but down it's three."

How long will the next
train to Glasgow be?
**About the same length as
the one you just missed.**

"Doctor, doctor,
I think I need glasses!"
**"You certainly do,
this is a fish shop!"**

"Doctor, doctor, I'm having
problems with my breathing!"
**"I'll soon put a
stop to that!"**

What do you get if you cross
a cow with a camel?
Lumpy milkshakes

How do fish communicate
with each other?
By sea-mail.

How do you start a bear race?
Say, "Ready, teddy, go!"

How do bears watch
Big Brother?
On a teddy-vision.

What's black and white
and red all over?
A panda with sunburn.

What happened to the
stupid tap-dancer?
He fell in the sink.

What do you call a panda
at the North Pole?
Lost.

Why does Father Christmas
come down chimneys?
Because it soots him.

What exams did
Father Christmas take
at school?
Ho, ho, ho levels.

What do you call a
man with a spade on
his head?
Doug.

What do you call a girl
with a cat on her head?
Kitty.

What relation is a doormat
to a doorstep?
A step farther.

What are dog biscuits
made from?
Collie flour.

What goes tick, tock, woof?
A watchdog.

"Doctor, doctor,
I think I'm invisible!"
"Who said that!"

"Doctor, doctor, I feel
like a trampoline!"
**"Sit down, stand up,
sit down."**

"Doctor, doctor,
I keep thinking I'm a dustbin!"
"Don't talk rubbish."

"Let's sit and wait for the cuckoo
to come out of the cuckoo clock."
**"I'd rather see
Grandad come out of the
grandfather clock."**

What do you call a
camel with three humps?
Humphrey.

What happens if you
eat Christmas decorations?
You get tinselitis.

How does Santa begin a joke?
**'This one will
sleigh you...'**

Yucky

What do you give a
seasick elephant?
Lots of room!

What's the difference
between a lavatory brush
and a chocolate biscuit?
**You can't dip a lavatory
brush in your tea.**

Knock, knock.
Who's there?
Luxembourg.
Luxemburg who?
**Luxembourg just did it
on your head!**

What's the difference between
tapioca pudding and frogspawn?
Not a lot!

"Is that steak pie I smell?"
"It is, and you do."

Why did the fish blush?
**Because it saw
the ship's bottom.**

"You had egg for breakfast,
I can see it on your chin."
**"No I didn't, that
was yesterday."**

What happens if you play table
tennis with a bad egg?
**First it goes ping,
then it goes pong.**

What kind of sandwich
speaks for itself?
A tongue sandwich.

Did you hear about the
boy scout whose beret
blew off in a field full of cows?
**He had to try on 20
before he found it!**

"Waiter! There's a worm
on my plate!"
**"That's not a worm, sir,
that's your sausage."**

"Waiter, there's a fly
in my soup."
**"Don't worry, sir,
it wiped its feet on
the bread roll."**

"Waiter, why have you got your
thumb on my apple pie?"
**"To stop it falling on the
floor again, madam."**

"Waiter, this fish
smells terrible."
**"Yes, it's a case of
long time, no sea."**

Knock, knock.
Who's there?
Sonia.
Sonia who?
**Sonia shoe,
I can smell it
from here.**

101

Knock, knock.
Who's there?
Nick.
Nick who?
Nick R. Elastic.

"How did Mum know you
hadn't had a bath?"
"I forgot to dirty the towel."

How many skunks does it
take to make a big stink?
A phew.

What animal do you look
like when you're in the bath?
A little bear.

Why do traffic lights turn red?
**Because they have to
stop and go in the
middle of the street.**

"Tom gave me his pig."
"You can't keep it here. What about
the smell?"
"The pig won't mind."

What's an ig?
**An eskimo's house
without a loo.**

What do you call a woman
with two lavatories on her head?
Lulu.

What's the best place
to have the school sick-room?
Next to the canteen!

What do you call little
white things in your head
that bite?
Teeth.

How can you catch dandruff?
**Shake your head over
a paper bag.**

What does the Queen do
when she burps?
Issues a Royal Pardon.

When does a bee fly
with its legs crossed?
**When it's looking
for a BP station.**

What makes snuffly
rock music?
Electric catarrh.

What can you do if your
nose goes on strike?
Picket.

"Your brother's built
upside down."

"What do you mean?"

**"His nose runs and his
feet smell."**

"What kind of bird
impressions do you do?"

"I eat worms."

How do you make anti-freeze?
Hide her winter woollies.

"Doctor, doctor, there's something
wrong with my stomach."

**"If you keep your
coat buttoned up
no one will notice."**

What do you do with
a sick horse?
Take it to horsepital.

What do you give a pony
that has a cold?
Cough stirrup.

"What are you giving your little
sister for Christmas?"
**"I'm not sure. Last year
I gave her chickenpox."**

"I was going to buy Grandad
a handkerchief for Christmas
but I didn't."
"Why not?"
**"I couldn't find one big
enough for his nose!"**

"Did you hear the joke
about the dirty T-shirt?"
"No."
"That's one on you!"

Why did the fish blush?
Because the seaweed.

"Waiter! Was that cottage pie?"
"Yes, sir."
**"Well, fetch a doctor,
I think I've just swallowed
a window!"**

"Waiter! This egg is bad!"
**"Don't blame me, sir, I only
laid the table!"**

"Waiter! What is that fly doing on my ice cream?"
"Learning to ski, sir."

How do you stop a skunk from smelling?
Cut off its nose.

What goes qq-thump, qq-thump, qq-thump?
A centipede with a wooden leg.

What do you get if you cross a skunk with an owl?
A bird that smells but doesn't give a hoot!

"Help! A shark's just bitten off my foot!"

"Which one?"

"How should I know, all sharks look the same to me."

"That film gave me a cold, slithery feeling down my neck."

"So that's where my ice cream went!"

"My friend said you weren't fit to live with pigs."

"And what did you say?"

"Oh, I stuck up for you. I said of course you were fit to live with pigs."

109

"Your dog's really lazy"

"Why do you say that?"

"Yesterday I watered the garden and he never lifted a leg to help me."

What's yellow, brown and hairy?

Cheese on toast dropped on the carpet.

Knock, knock.

Who's there?

Thumping.

Thumping who?

Thumping with lots of legs just crawled up your trousers.

What happened to the snake with a cold?

She adder viper nose.

Who wrote 'A Life on the Ocean Wave'?

Eva Lott.

What has a bottom
at the top?
A leg.

How can you stop your nose
running?
**Stick out your foot
and trip it up.**

What do you give
a pig with a rash?
Oinkment.

"Do you know anyone who's been on the telly?"
"My little brother did once but he can use a potty now."

What nut sounds
like a sneeze?
A cashew.

What do you get if you cross
a seagull with a parrot?
**A bird that poos on your
head and then says 'Sorry.'**

What do you get if you cross
a birthday cake with a tin of
baked beans?
**A cake that blows out
its own candles.**

What did one eye
say to the other?
**"Between us is something
that smells."**

Should you eat sausages with your fingers?
No, fingers should be eaten separately.

What do you get if you cross a skunk with a boomerang?
A bad smell you can't get rid of.

"What are you going to do with that horse manure?"
"Put it on my strawberries."
"Really? We put cream on ours!"

"Does your mum cook by gas or electricity?"
"I don't know, I've never tried to cook her."

"Is this cloudy Lemonade?"
"No, it's just the glass that's dirty."

What's a two-handed cheese?

One that you eat with one hand while you hold your nose with the other.

What's brown and sounds like a bell?

Dung.

What's brown and sticky?

A stick.

"Did you hear the story about the dustbin lorry?"

"Yes, it was a load of old rubbish."

Why can't a steam engine sit down?
Because it has a tender behind.

Have you heard the joke about the dirty window?
You wouldn't see through it!

"Do you know the way to Bath?"
"I always use soap and water."

"Do you always wash in dirty water?"
"It wasn't dirty when I started."

How can you make a tortoise fast?
Don't feed it.

"Waiter, waiter! Why is my steak pie all smashed up?"
"Well, you did ask me to step on it, sir."

What did the mayonnaise
say to the fridge?
**"Close the door,
I'm dressing."**

What do you get if you
cross a skunk with a wasp?
**Something that stinks
and stings.**

What's worse than a
giraffe with a stiff neck?
An elephant with a cold.

What airline do monsters
travel on?
British Scareways.

Why do you call your
brother Wonder Boy?
**People look at him
and wonder.**

"Have you ever had
your eyes checked?"
**"No, they've always
been blue."**

"Keep that dog out of the house, it's full of fleas."

"Rover, don't go in the house, it's full of fleas."

What happens when a flea is very angry?
It gets hopping mad.

What time of year is it when you sit on a drawing-pin?
Spring!

Why did the bald man stick his head
out of the window?
To get some fresh air.

What do frogs like to drink?
Croaka Cola.

Why did granny put her hands
to her mouth when she sneezed?
To catch her teeth.

"Waiter! What's this in my soup?"
**"I don't know, I can't tell one
insect from another."**

"I just swallowed a bone!"
"Are you choking?"
"No, I'm serious."

Knock, knock.
Who's there?
Alec.
Alec who?
**Alec Freddie but
I don't like you!**

What did the kebab say as it was
about to be put on the skewer?
"Spear me, spear me!"

What's a mushroom?
**A place where
school dinners are prepared.**

"You've got your shoes
on the wrong feet!"
**"But these are the
only feet I've got!"**

Knock, knock.
Who's there?
Victor.
Victor who?
**Victor his trousers
climbing the tree.**

What do you get if you pull your
knickers up to your armpits?
A chest of drawers.

What do you get if you cross
an alligator with a tummy bug?
An illigator.

"Waiter, there's a
dead fly in my soup!"
**"I'm afraid they
can't swim, sir."**

"Waiter! This food's
not fit for a pig!"
**"I'll bring you some
that is, sir."**

"Waiter, there's a
film on my soup!"
**"Have you seen
it before, sir?"**

"I don't like all the flies
in this restaurant."
**"Tell me which ones you
particularly dislike and I'll
have them thrown out."**

What's the best cure
for water on the knee?
Drainpipe trousers.

How can you find out
where a flea has bitten you?
You start from scratch.

How do you start
a flea race?
**"One, two,
flea - go!"**

Which British town
is known for its bad meat?
Oldham.

Where did the
sick ship go?
To the dock.

What's a slug?
**A snail with a
housing problem.**

Why did the skunk
take an aspirin?
**Because it had a
stinking cold.**

Why are skunks
always fighting?
They enjoy raising a stink.

"Why won't you take your
sister with you when you go
fishing?"
**"She eats all
my maggots."**

Did you hear about the
dog that lived on garlic?
**Its bark was worse
than its bite.**

Who wrote 'Living on
Garlic and Onions'?
I. Malone.

"Why have you got a sausage
behind your ear?"
**"Oh dear, I must have eaten
my pencil for lunch."**

123

What can you keep
even if you give it away?
A cold.

How can you stop a cold
in the head going to your chest?
Tie a knot in your neck!

"Did you hear the story
about the dustbin lorry?"
**"Yes, it was a load
of old rubbish."**

Knock, knock.
Who's there?
Stan.
Stan who?
**Stan back,
I'm going to sneeze!**

Why couldn't the young skunk have
a chemistry set for Christmas?
**His mother said it would
stink the house out.**

Knock, knock.

Who's there?

Pooh.

Pooh who?

Pooh, what an awful smell!

What is the smelliest city in America?

Phew York.

What do you get if you cross a bear with an old pair of socks?

Winnie the Pooh.

"Your socks have got holes in them!"

"How else would I get my feet in?"

"Is your bad tooth better now?"

"I don't know, I left it at the dentist."

125

"She has a heart of gold."
"It must match her teeth."

Why did Henry the eigth
have so many wives?
**He liked to chop
and change.**

Why did the mechanic
sleep under his car?
**Because he had to wake up
really oily in the morning.**

What was the first thing
Henry the eigth did when he came
to the throne?
He sat down.

"I've come to tune your piano."
"But we didn't send for you."
"No, but your neighbours did!"

What's the highest place on
earth you can go to the loo?
On the top of Mount Everest.

Knock, knock.
Who's there?
Ahab.
Ahab who?
**Ahab to go to the
loo in a hurry!**

Knock, knock.
Who's there?
Pencil.
Pencil who?
**Pencil fall down if
the elastic breaks!**